OUR WORLD IN COLOUR
BOMBAY AND GOA

OUR
WORLD IN
COLOUR
BOMBAY & GOA

Photography by
Alain Evrard and Luca I. Tettoni
Text by Rivka Israel

The Guidebook Company Limited

Distributors
Australia and New Zealand: The Book Company,
100 Old Pittwater Road, Brookvale, NSW 2100, Australia.

Canada: Prentice Hall Canada,
1870 Birchmount Road, Scarborough, Ontario MIP 257, Canada.

Hong Kong: China Guides Distribution Services Ltd.,
14 Ground Floor, Lower Kai Yuen Lane, North Point, Hong Kong.

India and Nepal: UBS Publishers' Distributors Ltd., 5 Ansari Road,
Post Box 7015, New Delhi 110 002, India.

Singapore and Malaysia: MPH Distributors (S) PTE Ltd., 601 Sims
Drive, No. 03/07-21, Pan-I Complex, Singapore 1438.

UK: Springfield Books Limited, Springfield House, Norman Road,
Dendy Dale, Huddersfield HD8 8TH, West Yorkshire, England.

USA: Publishers Group West Inc.,
4065 Hollis, Emeryville, CA 94608, USA.

Text and A–Z of Facts and Figures by Rivka Israel
Captions by Mandakani Dubey

Photography byAlain Evrard (2-3, 6-7, 10-11, 25, 32
bottom, 38 upper, 39 upper, 40, 41 lower, 42-3, 45-6
51 lower, 56 middle, 57-80 all)
Luca Invernizzi Tettoni (5,16-24 all, 26-31, 32 top middle, 33,
36 top, lower left, lower right, 37 top, 38 lower, 39 lower,
41 upper, 44, 47, 48-49 all, 50 upper, 52-55 all, 56 top and bottom)
Dallas and John Heaton Photobank (8-9, 12-13, 17, 34-35)

Edited by Nick Wallwork
Series Editor: Rose Borton
Photo Editor: Caroline Robertson
Artwork by Aubrey Tse, Au Yeung Chui Kwai

Printed in Hong Kong

ISBN 962-217-147-8

Title spread
*Most of the people of this
hamlet on the banks of the
Zuari River earn a modest
living from the gifts of nature—
fish and coconuts.*

Right
*Near the junction of Mahatma
Gandhi and Dadabhai Naoroji
Roads, a BEST double decker
bus halts to pick up passengers.
BEST is rightly prided by
Bombayites as being the
country's best city transport
system. Close by is an old Parsi
well, the man with the water-
cart is probably on his way
there to collect water for sale
in the city.*

Pages 6–7
*The main crop of Goa is rice
and the whole region abounds
with green fields such
as this one, at Cortalim. By the
end of September it will be a
beautiful golden-yellow.*

Pages 8–9
*At Apollo Bunder you should
sit a while on the wall near
the Gateway of India before
boarding the launch to
Elephanta. Behind the
Gateway is the older Taj
Mahal Hotel— the Sea Lounge
at the hotel is a delightful
place, especially if you can
get a window seat.*

Pages 10–11
*Fishing has always been the
main source of income for the
Goan population, even after
the onslaught of the tourist
industry. At Calangute Beach,
fishermen set off early for their
day's work.*

Pages 12–13
*This camel parading up and
down Juhu Beach at sunrise is
popular both with Bombayites
and foreign tourists. A camel
ride is a bumpy and enjoyable
experience, but make sure you
settle both distance and price
with the camel-driver before
starting out!*

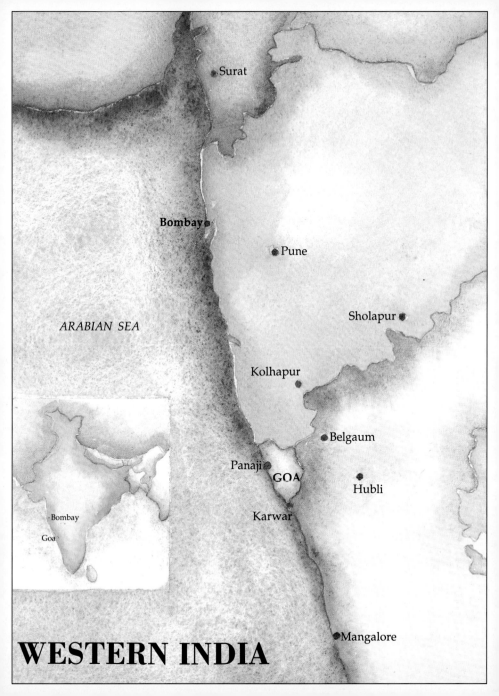

Surat

Bombay

Pune

ARABIAN SEA

Sholapur

Kolhapur

Belgaum

Panaji

GOA

Hubli

Karwar

Bombay

Goa

Mangalore

WESTERN INDIA

INTRODUCTION

BOMBAY is not a city that leaves you indifferent—you either love it, or hate it. And if you are one of the nine million people for whom this narrow strip of land is home, you belong to it absolutely. Bombay's people make it different from any other Indian city: coming from far-flung parts of the country, they have woven their various faiths, customs, cultures and languages into the life of the city, giving it a character all of its own.

Its climate is generally a kind one, but the monsoons can cause considerable distress: hut and pavement dwellings are often destroyed by the continuous downpour. Roads and railways are flooded out of operation, and Bombayites think nothing of wading through knee-deep water to get to work on time. Humidity is uncomfortably high throughout the year, but the cool sea-breeze brings welcome relief, more than compensating for the sweat, grit and grime of this crowded city.

Bombay's beautiful coastline is probably its most outstanding feature. Its importance is reflected in the traditional occupation of the Kolis, the natives of the region, who continue to live in their close-knit fishing communities. The Kolis still retain their identity, most noticeably in their dialect and style of dress. Their ancestors are said to have settled on the cluster of seven islands, which later became Bombay, in the first century AD. The other early inhabitants of these islands were the Bhandaris. These people were rice cultivators and distillers of toddy—a powerful liquor made from palm sap.

The islands of Bombay survive today only as place names in the city: Colaba, Dongri, Mazagaon, Girgaum, Worli, Mahim and Pare-Sion. These islands were ruled by various Hindu rajas until 1401, when they came under the control of the Sultans of Gujarat. In 1534, the Muslim ruler submitted to the superior force of the Portuguese, to whom he ceded the port of Bassein (Vasai), along with the seven islands and Salsette. Bombay's Roman Catholics and their churches are the legacy of this period. Though modernization has robbed many of the churches of their Portuguese-style facades, some fine examples still survive. One of these is St Andrew's Church in Bandra. Both on the main island and on Salsette (most of which is now part of Greater Bombay) there are some minor remains of Portuguese fortifications. At Bassein the ruins of a walled settlement, including a large church, are well worth a visit.

The Portuguese called the seven islands Bom Bahia, meaning 'good bay' and this may have given Bombay its name. Some scholars believe that the name derives from King Bhimadeva, also known as Bimba, who built settlements on Mahim Island in 1294. However, the most widely accepted theory is that Bombay (Mumbai in Marathi) owes its name to the goddess Mumba Devi who is worshipped by the Kolis. The temple of Mumba Devi once stood in the area now occupied by the Victoria Terminus before it was moved to Paidhoni in central Bombay in the 18th century.

Under the Portuguese, Bombay remained an obscure archipelago surrounded by marshes and swamps. Only about 10,000 people lived there in 1661, when it was acquired by the British as part of the dowry of Catherine of Braganza on her mar-

The ornate style of the Old Taj Mahal Hotel on Apollo Bunder (top), contrasts with the newer and much plainer highrise buildings of the city (above).

riage to Charles II. The gift was not highly thought of, and by 1668 the Crown had leased Bombay to the East India Company for £10 sterling a year!

The Company soon recognized Bombay's potential. Under far-sighted governors like Gerald Aungier, the construction of the city and harbour was started and Bombay began to emerge as a centre of trade. During the 18th century growth was gradual, but the 1800s saw rapid commercial and industrial development. The power of the Marathas who ruled the inland area had dwindled, and in 1818 the British annexed the territories of the Peshwar. The building of India's roads and railways strengthened Bombay's ties with the mainland and the opening of the Suez Canal in 1869 finally established Bombay as India's gateway to the West.

During this period Bombay became an important 'cottonopolis'. The short-stapled cotton of Gujarat, though of inferior quality, was cheaper than the long-stapled American variety, and the cotton mills of northern England had a growing need for the raw material. In 1861, when the Civil War broke out in America and cotton supplies were cut off, it was the Indian merchants who benefited.

The enterprising and determined businessmen of Bombay soon decided that it made sense to set up their own mills locally. By 1900 there were about 90 cotton mills in the city, and the industry has been an important source of employment for Bombay's people ever since. In the last decade or so, however, the mills have been in the doldrums: in addition to having to function with obsolete machinery, they have also been the victims of strikes and government indifference.

The British, unlike the Portuguese, showed religious tolerance, and Bombay's growing prosperity attracted people of many religions and regions to the city. The inflow continues to this day and is now a source of concern to the city authorities. The city limits have been extended further north, and a twin city—New Bombay—is being developed across the harbour, in Vashi.

Bombay is home to almost every major world religion. Hindus, Muslims and Christians are the larger groups, with smaller communities of Sikhs, Jains, Buddhists (mainly followers of the late Dr B R Ambedkar, outstanding leader of the former 'Untouchables'), Parsis and even Jews.

The Hindu population of Bombay is largely Marathi-speaking, or Maharashtrian (though technically every Bombayite is a Maharashtrian, this term has come to denote a person whose mother tongue is Marathi). There are also a significant number of Gujaratis who dominate the stock exchange and the cotton, gold, silver and diamond markets. In 1947 there was an influx of Hindu refugees from Sind in Pakistan, many of whom settled in Ulhasnagar, north of Bombay. Today a generous share of Bombay's business and money is controlled by the Sindhis.

Bombay's Muslims belong to various sects. Both Shiahs and Sunnis are present in substantial numbers, and the Shiahs are further divided into the Bohras and the Khojas. Of the Khojas, a large proportion are followers of the Aga Khan. There are areas in the city which are recognizably Muslim, mainly around the mosques. The Mohamed Ali Road area of south Bombay, where many Muslims live and carry on their trade, is one of the most fascinating parts of the city. Wander down the bylanes to Bhendi Bazaar or Chor Bazaar, and you will find shops selling everything from 'antiques', furniture, clothes and jewellery, to hardware, ceramics, leather goods, attar (perfume) and delicious biryani, kebabs rolled up in roti, and hot, sweet jalebis.

Most of Bombay's Christians are Roman Catholics—Goans, East Indians from Salsette Island and Bassein, and Mangaloreans from Karnataka. Most Catholics speak English, Konkani or Marathi. There are also the Malayalam–speaking Syrian Christians and smaller groups from Kerala, who belong to the Greek Orthodox Church.

The followers of Zarathusthra fled to India more than a thousand years ago to escape persecution in Persia. Their first settlement was in Gujarat, and the Parsis speak their own, endearing form of Gujarati. They moved to Bombay in large numbers in the 1800s and invested heavily in Bombay's dockyards and shipping. They were also among the city's first industrialists. Their contribution to India as a whole, and to Bombay in particular, has been out of proportion to their numbers. Industry, science and medical research, along with the arts, have all benefited from Parsi talent, initiative and wealth.

Bombay also has a community of 'Iranis'—both Muslim and Parsi. In an Irani restaurant you can relax with a hot cup of strong, sweet tea, or have an omelette and toast, or even a full meal, for a reasonable price. These restaurants with their old fashioned chairs, marble-topped tables and mirrors are unique to Bombay. Alas, their numbers are dwindling.

Even the tiny community of Jews in Bombay is divided into two sections. The larger group, the Bene Israel, claims descent from the survivors of a shipwreck on the Konkan coast south of Bombay in the second century BC. They look and dress like the Maharashtrians, and their language is Marathi. In contrast, the 'Baghdadi' Jews, who came to Bombay as merchants in the 18th and 19th centuries, are distinctly non-Indian in appearance. Today the number of Baghdadi Jews is very small, but the wealth of families like the Sassoons made lasting contributions to mills, docks, libraries, the health services and science education in the city.

While Marathi (along with English) is the official language, the Bombay Municipal Corporation provides primary and secondary education in at least ten languages. Apart from Hindi—the national language—Urdu, Gujarati, Tamil, Telugu, Malayalam, Sindhi and Konkani are also spoken in Bombay. The resourceful people of Bombay have overcome Babel by developing a local lingo—a random mixture of Hindi, Marathi, Gujarati and English—which is a source of amusement, or horror, to other Indians. This hybrid has been widely caricatured in Hindi films.

Places of worship dot the city. For Hindus there is the Walkeshwar temple complex at Malabar Hill, which dates back to the 11th century. Devotees take regular ritual dips in its sacred tank, the Banganga, whose waters are said to have sprung out of the earth as the arrow of Lord Rama pierced it. Particularly sacred to the Hindu business community is the Mahalakshmi Temple, dedicated to Lakshmi, goddess of wealth. Like Walkeshwar, this temple stands by the sea.

In the sea just north of Mahalakshmi stands the island mosque of the Muslim

The Gateway of India (top) is Bombay's best-known landmark, and always the centre of activity. This Arc de Triomphe was built as a monument to the British conquest of India. (Above) The tomb of Haji Ali stands on a rocky outcrop jutting into the sea. The body of this Muslim saint is exquisitely entombed in a semi-circular cenotaph and draws people of all faiths.

The Zakaria Mosque.

saint, Haji Ali. At low tide one can walk across the narrow causeway which links it to the mainland. The Raudat Tahera mosque in the crowded Bhendi Bazaar is a more recent and lavishly decorated embodiment of the faith of the local Muslim businessmen.

A Buddhist temple stands at Worli, and the main Jain temple is at Back Bay, at the southern end of the city. The Parsis keep their sacred fire burning in fire temples which are closed to non-Parsis. As the Parsis hold both fire and earth sacred, neither cremation nor burial of the dead is permitted to them. The Tower of Silence on Malabar Hill is the place where the Parsis expose their dead to vultures and the elements.

In Colaba stands the Afghan memorial church of St John the Evangelist. This beautiful structure with its Gothic arches and stained-glass windows was consecrated in 1858 as a memorial to the lives lost in the first Afghan War. The Anglican Cathedral of St Thomas, which stands near Horniman Circle in south Bombay boasts a bishop, but today sees more tourists than worshippers.

South Bombay boasts several fine examples of colonial architecture, most of which date to the second half of the 19th century, when Bombay's new-found wealth was invested in civic and commercial buildings. Perhaps the finest structure among these is the Victoria Terminus (VT) and the adjoining Central Railway Headquarters. Designed by Frederic William Stevens, this High-Victorian Gothic masterpiece is built of sandstone and granite, with blue-grey basalt decorations within.

George Wittet left his mark on Bombay in the early 1900s. The sandstone-and-basalt Prince of Wales Museum with its dome and other oriental features is among the most important museums in India. It contains some fine Mughal and Rajasthani miniature paintings, and pieces of jade and chinaware. But Wittet is most remembered for the Gateway of India at Apollo Bunder. Through this magnificent triumphal arch George V and Queen Mary entered India in 1911, the year of the Delhi Durbar, and through this arch, also, did the last of the British troops leave India.

For those with an interest in ancient monuments Bombay admittedly has little to offer. An hour's ride away from Apollo Bunder by motor-launch is the island of Gharapuri, renamed Elephanta by the Portuguese (the massive stone elephant that once stood on the island is now in the gardens of the Bombay Zoo). The impressive rock-cut cave temples of Elephanta were excavated in the seventh and eighth centuries. About 45 km (28 miles) to the north of Apollo Bunder, in the suburb of Borivali, is a National Park. Here are the hill caves of Kanheri which have Buddhist sculptures, again on a large scale, dating back to about the second century.

Bombay's transport system is an efficient one, given the numbers that it serves. The old-fashioned horse-drawn Victorias, or ghoda-gadis, have all but disappeared, though you can still take a cool evening ride down the crowded Colaba Causeway to Apollo Bunder. Black and yellow taxis with their reckless but skilful drivers wait at every corner or can be flagged on the run. In the suburbs, auto-rickshaws offer you a rather bumpy ride at a lower price. But the arteries of the city are the BEST buses and local train services. Though crowded, the trains and buses of Bombay can get you to any place for a reasonable fare. A local train at the rush hour is a terrifying sight with people bursting out of every door. But the speed and relative regularity of the trains make up for the discomfort.

Like any other metropolis, Bombay has the usual assortment of fancy restaurants, but fast food, Indian-style, is its real forte. One never has to walk far to find food to suit one's taste and pocket—South Indian or Gujarati vegetarian thalis, pau bhaji, mutton or chicken biryani—and even 'Chinese' fare is available at little roadside stalls or restaurants. For those who prefer to have warm, home-cooked lunch delivered to their place of work, there is the faithful band of dabbawallas, unique to Bombay. Using local trains, they ferry dabbas between homes and offices or factories with surprising efficiency.

Inevitably, Bombay is a difficult place in which to live. The central areas of the city are crowded with chawls (tenement buildings), where large families live together in single rooms. The still less fortunate build their homes of tin, plywood and plastic sheets wherever they can manage to establish themselves. Even a tiny space in a slum commands a price and is a source of income for a 'slum-lord'. These pockets of extreme poverty stand out in frightening contrast to the prosperity all around. The evils of child labour and the growing power of organized crime are evident in every part of the city. But as long as Bombay offers some hope of employment people will continue to pour into the city, determined to stay there under any circumstances.

Statues of benevolent donors can be seen in parks throughout Bombay.

However involved they might be in the daily struggle of earning a living, people in Bombay are always enthusiastic about entertainment. Both traditional and modern Marathi drama attract large crowds at Shivaji Mandir in Dadar. Hindi, Gujarati and English theatres also flourish. A recent addition to the scene is Pithvi Theatre in Juhu, set up by Shashi and Jennifer Kapoor (the Kapoors are the most famous film family in Bombay). The Prithvi Theatre, named after Prithviraj Kapoor, is built in the style of an old Shakespearean theatre, with a round stage.

Bombay is the city in which the largest number of films in a single language—Hindi—are made. The glamorous lifestyles of film stars are a never-failing source of interest to the people, and film magazines enjoy brisk sales. The Hindi film is part of Bombay's hotchpotch culture, a ridiculous mixture of Western style and Indian tradition. In the words of Salman Rushdie, the Bombay-born novelist, 'Bombay was a culture of remakes . . . its cinema endlessly re–invented *The Magnificent Seven* and *Love Story*, obliging all its heroes to save at least one village from murderous dacoits and all its heroines to die of leukemia at least once in their careers, preferably at the start'.

There are a number of playing fields or *maidans* in Bombay, where budding Gavaskars crowd for cricket practice, however, parks and gardens in the city are lamentably few. One of the nicest of these, the Hanging Gardens on Malabar Hill, enjoys a superb panoramic view of the city. For weekend trips, Matheran, Lonavala and Khandala in the hills near Bombay are popular places, but it is the beaches which are the most popular with visitors. Marve Madh Island and Gorai beaches are more remote, but even there it is difficult to find a quiet spot on a holiday weekend.

After a day's work, many people take a stroll down the sea-front. The most popular places are Marine Drive, Chowpatty (where the bhelpuri , Malai kulfi and coconut water, combined with the sea air, taste delicious), on the rocks at Land's End at Bandra, or on the sands of Juhu. All these places stay awake, as does the whole city, late into the night. In the early hours of morning, when the last stragglers are making their way home, the city snatches a few hour's sleep.

Goa

One of the most enjoyable trips you can make from Bombay is the boat trip down to Goa. You board at Bhaucha Dhakka (literally Brother's Wharf) and the journey takes about 24 hours. The trip provides an excellent foretaste of the holiday you can look forward to at the other end—pleasant and unhurried. However, if you have neither time nor patience, you can go by coach or plane (the train journey is ridiculously long and complicated).

Goa, the land of white churches, sunny beaches, song, dance and the potent cashew feni, is a fascinating example of the harmonious coexistence of two distinct cultures, Latin and Indian. Today Goa is a state in the Union of India, 3,500 sq km (1,350 sq miles) of fertile land, watered by rivers, nestling between Maharashtra and Karnataka on the west coast. It is an area with plenty of rice fields, fruit and nut groves, and rich deposits of iron and manganese ores.

The Goans are an easy–going and hospitable people who still view the afternoon siesta as an important part of the day. The old Portuguese-style houses with their wide verandas and porches are made for family and social life, and graceful coconut palms and banana trees add to the sense of peace.

When Vasco da Gama came to India in 1498, 'seeking Christians and spices', Goa (or Govarashtra, the old name for South Konkan) was an important port of the kingdom of Vijayanagar. By the early years of the 16th century, however, Goa had been occupied by the Muslim kingdoms of Bijapur and Golconda. The Portuguese met with stiff resistance from the Muslim sultans, who were determined to maintain their monopoly of the spice trade. But equally determined was Alfonso de Albuquerque, a nobleman sent to the Indies to establish the Portuguese presence there. Not satisfied with two forts at Cochin and Cannanore, Albuquerque turned his attention to Goa and its fine natural harbour. He successfully attacked the fortress of Panjim from the sea and, after a fierce battle, Goa surrendered to the Portuguese on 25 November 1510, on the feast of St Catherine.

For the next four and a half centuries Goa remained Portuguese India. Portugal's empire declined, the British came and went, India became a republic, and Goa continued its peaceful existence, virtually untouched by the political turbulence which surrounded it. In 1961 Goa was finally absorbed into the India Union. With Daman and Diu (smaller Portuguese territories to the north) it formed a union territory. People from other parts of the country began to migrate into Goa, and this brought a certain amount of change. In 1987 Goa's wish to be recognized as a full-

The population of Goa is predominantly Christian— a reminder of her sixteenth century conquest by Portugal. Hindus and Christians live together amicably and participate with gusto in each other's festivals. The Hindu temples in Goa such as this one, are distinguished by their lamp pillars.

fledged Indian state was fulfilled.

Portugal's military and mercantile domination brought with it religious zeal and intolerance. Large numbers of Goans were converted to Christianity, first by the Franciscans, and then by the Jesuits who were led by St Francis Xavier, later to become Goa's patron saint. Most converts took Portuguese names; thus, de Souza, da Costa, da Silva, Almeida, Pereira and Dias are common among Catholic Goans. Some elderly Goans still speak Portuguese, though English has taken over, and Konkani is the state's official language. The Latin influence is very obvious in the Goan lifestyle and culture, music and dance. However, the people of Goa, Hindu or Christian, are undoubtedly of Indian stock.

The centre of Portuguese Goa—Goa Doraido or Golden Goa—lay deep in the estuary of the Mandovi River—a magnificent city of churches, palaces, stately buildings and wide streets. The city reached its zenith in the 16th and 17th centuries when it was known as the 'Rome of the Orient'. Today it is called Old Goa: an historic site which has been put in the care of the Archaeological Survey of India. The only inhabitants are ecclesiastics and students. Many of the fine buildings have fallen into ruin, and most have disappeared without trace. Still, no holiday in Goa is complete without a ramble through the old city.

The Cathedral (Cathedral of St Catherine) was built over a period of 57 years and provides a splendid example of Renaissance architecture. It is the largest Christian church in Asia and the interior is beautifully decorated with intricate floral frescos which combine Indian and European styles. With its imposing façade, it is the finest piece of Baroque architecture in India. Regular services are held in the church and the atmosphere of fervent devotion within is overwhelming. But it is the little chapel, not immediately visible, to which pilgrims are drawn—the chapel which houses the tomb of St Francis Xavier. The tomb originally came from Italy as a gift from the Grand Duke of Tuscany. The saint's body, which was brought to Goa almost 150 years after his death, lies in an airtight glass coffin within a silver casket crafted by Goan silversmiths.

Goa's charm is not, however, confined to its Portuguese relics. Many who come to this peace-lover's paradise spend all their days on the golden beaches that form Goa's western fringe. In the north are the idyllic Vagator and Anjuna beaches. Vagator stands in the shadow of Chapora Fort, serene and secluded, while Anjuna has become the adopted home of hippies, providing them with the perfect escape from Western civilization.

It is an easy climb over the low hill separating Anjuna from Candolim (also known as Baga). The beaches of Candolim and Calangute form a stretch of sand north of Aguada Fort and not far from Panjim. Though still enchanting, they are more obviously developed, with plenty of souvenir stalls, hotels and resorts. Holiday accommodation is also available in the many small houses in the coconut groves behind these beaches. Quaint little restaurants, often located in shacks or beach huts, serve seafood of every description cooked in delicious Goan curries and sauces.

Miramar, the beach of Panjim town, is rather less inspiring, but at the rocky

Goan architecture has a heavy Iberian influence, shown here in the detail of a Portuguese ship in one of Goa's many churches.

A small wayside shrine (top) silhouetted enchantingly against the sky reflects Goa at its most quaint, peaceful and charming; the different cultural influences that have shaped Goa are evident not just in its churches and palaces but also in the smaller residential buildings (above).

Opposite page
Hindi film actress Tina Munim relaxes between takes—the portrayal of women on the Hindi screen is often crassly sexist, which is perhaps one reason for the popular appeal of these films in India's largely patriachal society.

point between the mouths of the Mandovi and Zuari rivers lies the tiny bay of Dona Paula, where the dark sand makes a beautiful contrast with the amazing blue of the sea. For those who prefer something more secluded, the picturesque beaches of Betul and Palolem, where nature continues to have full rein, remain relatively free from the pressures of tourism.

Towns in Goa are few and small by Indian standards. The capital, Panaji or Panjim, on the southern bank of the Mandovi River, has a population of about 80,000. On the Strand or Campal, facing the river, stands the Secretariat built by the Portuguese in 1615. This was formerly the site of the palace of the 'Idalcan', Ismail Adil Shah, after which the Largo di Palacio (Palace Square) was named. For a change from the usual statues of political and military figures, visitors can see the statue of the Goan Abbé Faria (1755–1819). Faria was a hypnotist who travelled to Portugal, Italy and France where he is said to have been influenced by Franz Anton Mesmer.

But the soul of Goa lies in its sleepy little villages which sit contentedly amidst gentle hills, lazy rivers and lush vegetation. Most Goans live in villages and travel to town for business. Village houses are often large, always freshly painted, with wide verandas or porches, and surrounded by banana trees. Many houses are built of the commonly found laterite stone, and one still sees window panes of oyster shell, traditionally used instead of glass. Old-fashioned Goan furniture of heavy, ornately-carved wood has pride of place in many drawing rooms.

Religious faith is in evidence at every turn. Riding through the countryside, you are constantly aware of the little churches, shrines and crosses that dot the landscape. Each village has its local patron saint whose feast day is observed with traditional ceremony and gaiety.

Today Christian and Hindu customs and traditions mingle happily, but it was not always so. The first two centuries of Portuguese rule saw the systematic demolition of Hindu temples. This explains why the beautiful temples of Goa go back no further than the 19th century, and why most of them are found away from the coast in sheltered, wooded surroundings.

The Mangesh Temple (dedicated to Lord Shiva), the Shanta-Durga Temple and the Nagesh Temple are all in the neighbourhood of Ponda, a market town in what could be called the main Hindu-populated area of Goa. Architecturally the temples exhibit Portuguese as well as Islamic influence, though the courtyards and structures around them are distinctly Hindu. A unique feature is the deepmal, a several-storeyed lamp tower.

Goa is at its best from October to March. While festivity and celebration are an integral part of Goan life all year round, Christmas time is particularly joyful. This is closely followed in February and March by Carnival time. For three whole days all Goa makes merry—floats and displays lead the processions, children and grown-ups in fancy dress sing and dance in the streets and everyone has their share of fun, food and *feni*.

Above and left
Not all Bombay's brokers operate within the impersonal, modernistic skyscraper that houses the Stock Exchange; the teeming activity on the pavements outside probably accounts for a hefty percentage of the deals made.

Above and right
Thousands of people every day are absorbed into the fabric of this densely populated city. Commuting can be a nightmare, and newcomers have to be extremely resilient. However, the crush and noise is not as bad as it looks, provided you watch out for pickpockets!

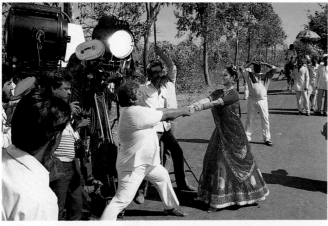

Bombay boasts the largest film industry in the world, specializing in huge potboilers with a bit of everything thrown in—romance, violence, comedy, drama. Stereotyped dramatic figures are regularly depicted, such as the damsel in distress, the macho cowboy-hero, the lusting villain, the long-suffering mother, the vamp who tries to entrap the hero, the good brother who dies: in fact, just about every cliché possible. Small wonder then that the advertising is about as subtle as the films themselves. Garish film posters such as these adorn almost every street corner in Bombay.

Following page
The Prince of Wales Museum was built to honour George V's first visit to India, it has a fine collection of oil paintings and Chinese jade pieces. The Natural History section is also well worth visiting.

Right
The Parsi community is almost exclusively Bombay-centred and is a major force in the commercial, cultural and social aspects of the city; Zoroastrian religious figures decorate Parsi fire temples and shrines which are dotted about Bombay.

Left
Inside the Asiatic Society Library, which is almost two centuries old, efforts are underway to reorganize and restore its many rare books.

Below
The library foyer is an architecturally impressive part of the building with its high ceiling and iron balustrade; below the steps is a statue of Sir Jugonnath Sunkersett, a leading sethia of Bombay's goldsmith community (1802-65).

Bottom
On the first floor stand images of various British governors of Bombay, one of them being Lord Elphinstone.

Above and left
Manhattan, perhaps? Two views of South Bombay show one of the most exciting parts of the city. In both pictures it is possible to see the Rajabai clock tower of Bombay University.

Opposite page
Nariman Point (top), a concrete jungle built on reclaimed land is one of Bombay's major business centres. The jelly-shaped building in the centre is the Vidhan Sabha, Maharashtra's Legislative Assembly.

Right
Another type of commercial activity altogether takes place in the residential/market areas of old Bombay. These older sections of the city have managed to retain the quaint, irresistible charm of Bombay.

Named after India's famous tourist attraction, the Taj Mahal Hotel has in some ways become a legend in its own right. This beautiful old building is said to have accidentally been built facing the wrong way, but this has not prevented it from enjoying a gorgeous view of the sea. (Below) One of the magnificently ornate dining rooms at the Taj. (Bottom) Guests receive a welcoming smile at the Taj Mahal Intercontinental, a more contemporary addition to the old hotel.

Right
A piece of the Raj in Bombay: the Victoria Terminus by night is an awe-inspiring sight. The headquarters of the Central Railways, this building is understandably the pride of Bombay. Opposite stands the Municipal Corporation building, designed by the same architect. (Below) The statue of Pherozeshah Mehta, in front of the Municipal Corporation building, towers benignly over the milling crowds. Mehta was one of the most highly respected citizens of Bombay, having made a lasting contribution to civic welfare while he was President of the Municipal Corporation. In fact, his impact was felt not just by the city of Bombay but by the entire country.

Scenes from the Elephanta Caves near Bombay. Elephanta is an island with several spectacular rock–cut caves that date back to between the 4th and 9th centuries AD; the massive trinity or **trimurti** *shown above depicts the three faces of Siva as the Creator, the Preserver and the Destroyer. The two gatekeepers on each side add an interesting touch.*

Mani Bhavan is where Mohandas Karamchand Gandhi, the 'Father of the Nation', stayed during his visits to Bombay in the early part of the Freedom struggle. It is historically significant since Gandhi launched many important movements from this house and even learnt how to spin his famous charkha here. It is now an excellent museum which depicts his life through photographs, films, taped speeches and letters; there is an exhaustive library with over 20,000 books on this extraordinary man.

45

Life along the banks of the Mandovi River has changed little over the last two centuries.

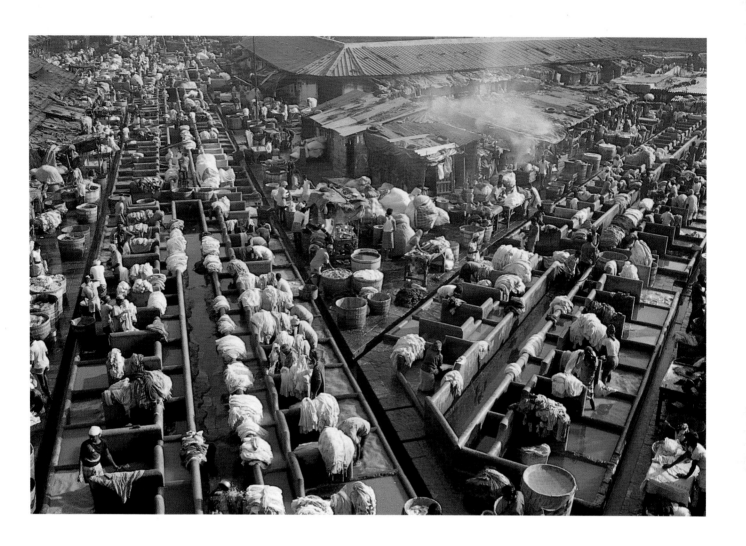

Above
*Dhobis provide an efficient
laundry service, although
their methods are hard on the
clothes they wash. Washing
machines are becoming more
and more popular with some
people but this has yet to really
affect the dhobi population.*

Right
*Lunch for most offices is
provided by the dabbawalas
who are unique to Bombay.
The dabbawalas use colour
codes to transport
home–cooked lunches to
waiting businesspeople.
Complicated though it sounds,
the lunch always reaches the
desired destination.*

Street hoardings are abundant in Bombay, and can be unwittingly hilarious; the one above with its lurid background and unusual spellings, is probably aimed at people who wish to move to the Gulf countries in search of employment.

Right
Film posters such as this one all have a target audience. This one is obviously meant to appeal to the more religious-minded, since it depicts Maharastra's favourite deity, Ganesh.

Centre right
This newspaper hoarding, startling in content, is regularly updated, in contrast to the 'Rainbow Electronics' board (far right), which looks forlorn and forgotten.

Below
A ghoda-gadi *(horse and carriage)* in a
Colaba sidestreet. The owner is probably
relaxing inside while the horses rest outside
until the next customer arrives to be 'taken
for a ride'!

Left
The donor and the beneficiary. Bombay's business community prides itself on its philanthropy; several institutes, schools and corporations bear family names or busts like this one in testimony of their self-imposed civic duty.

Above
The clubs of Bombay, such as the Bombay Gymkhana shown here, are extremely popular and have a long waiting list. The playing fields are still trimmed as carefully as they were in the erstwhile days of the Raj, when the clubs were set up by the British in order to recapture the flavour of 'home'.

Right
Father and son enjoy a glass of chai, hot milky tea, a popular refreshment at any time of the year.

Above
The secular and the sacred blend harmoniously outside temples and mosques where pilgrims camp, often after travelling great distances. Flowers and prasad, *food which has been blessed, are sold to worshippers who then offer them inside the shrine.*

Left
Priests perform a devotional service in front of the presiding deity in a Hindu temple; offerings of fruit and flowers are arranged around the deity while the flames of devotional lamps light up the sacred interior.

As in all towns and cities of India, the bazaars of Bombay are full of variety, colour and noise. Chaotic, but a never-ending source of interest for the visitor. An old woman (left) minds the family bookstore; on display are photographs of Indian film stars and inexpensive romantic novels. Pavement vendors (above) sell brightly coloured posters of mythological events and heroes. These pictures, sometimes referred to as 'calendar art', are inexpensive,very popular and usually adorn the walls of low-income homes, offices and restaurants.

Bombay is the fashion capital of India, with an active design and merchandising industry. A mannequin (below) lures customers into a shop with her sari of fine gold and white silk; Muslim women (bottom) often observe purdah, wearing long black gowns and veils in public; these Muslims with faces uncovered, stroll through one of the city's open air markets near a mosque. In days gone by elephants (right) were tamed for warfare and heavy work. Today they earn a little money for their owners by providing joy rides. Elephants are loved and revered because of their association with the elephant-headed deity Ganesh, touching or even seeing one is considered good luck. (Below right) A private dance performance in one of the city's steamier clubs imitates the elegant nautch of the courtesans of another era.

An evening stroll along the beach is popular with many of Bombay's residents since it is a beautiful sight even in this crowded metropolis. These residential apartments (left) are considered 'exclusive' since they are on the waterfront. The Haji Ali Mausoleum (below) has a dramatic offshore location, opposite the Mahalaxmi racecourse; during high tide the connecting causeway is submerged in water giving the impression that the mosque and tomb are floating out at sea in splendid isolation. Seagulls (bottom) are a common sight in Bombay as they hover over the water in search of food. As the sun rises over Bombay, they are the only inhabitants of this beach apart from a few yoga enthusiasts.

Opposite page
Marine Drive or Netaji Subhash Road, starts along Chowpatty Beach and winds up at the elite business district of Nariman Point; this wide boulevard is frequented by pedestrians, for whom a special walkway has been constructed along the seafront; the road glitters with street lights at night, earning for itself the sobriquet 'Queen's Necklace'.

Following page
Early morning at Baga beach. This tropical dream come true is one of the quieter beaches of Goa, where fishermen continue to ply their trade untroubled by rambunctious tourists. Baga even has a retreat for pilgrims and priests.

Fruit sellers at Panaji and Calangute beach. That pile of oranges (right) probably started out as a perfect pyramid, but in the fierce heat fruit is the most refreshing thing to eat. Children are expected to help earn a living from a fairly young age, they do, however, get a chance to put their feet up at times!

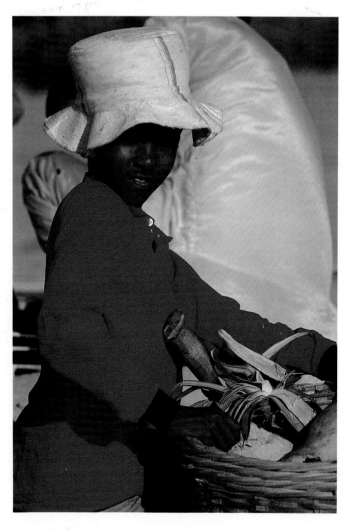

St. FRANCIS XAVIER

SATCHIT 89

Religion is omnipresent in Goa. St Francis Xavier is revered as its patron saint, since he came here as part of his travels around the East. (Top left) a representation of the saint at Baga beach. Old Goa is 10 km (6 miles) away from Panaji, where the Viceroy made his home, building palaces and villas for the gentry. The ceremonial entry to the city is made through the Viceroy's Arch, built by the great grandson of Vasco da Gama. The details of the Arch are well worth inspecting since they all have little stories of their own (above). The new buildings in Goa lack the majesty and beauty of the older structures; shown here (bottom left) is the detail of a recently built temple in Calangute, colourful if a little crass.

Right
To some, Goa is known as the 'Land of the White Churches', the Church of Immaculate Conception in Panaji has retained its pristine aura since it was built in 1541. This tall facade was the first indication of land for the sailors who travelled from Lisbon to Goa.

The popular perception of the Goan people is that of a fun-loving, carnival lot who live for festivals and tips from tourists. This is not altogether true, for although they do enjoy their feni, the Goans work hard at their traditional occupation of fishing.

A tribal woman in all her customary finery adds some more colour
to this already psychedelic lotus-eater's paradise; the silver earrings
and bead necklaces are exquisite to look at, but if you look closely
you will see that the pride of place is occupied by a set of keys!
A schoolgirl (right) chewing at her handkerchief studies the
camera with a mixture of caution, suspicion and interest.

The sea at Calangute Beach provides a cheap and effective means for this woman to wash her cattle. Despite the fact that Goa is predominantly Christian, cows are revered here as in other parts of the country, for Hindu traditions have survived to a large extent.

*The Mandovi River is the most famous
of Goa's ten rivers. The rickety but
ubiquitous ferry transports a fairly large
number of people on motorcycles, scooters,
bicycles or just on foot across the river.*

Religion permeates to the most basic levels for the Goans. This simple boat is 'blessed' by a painting of the Virgin Mother, which serves as a talisman. Their faith helps the fishermen believe that they can withstand strong currents and storms out at sea, and that they will get a good catch. A young fisherman (right) poses against his boat. Since they start young, most fishermen have a deep knowledge of the sea.

The rice fields of Goa add a lovely touch of green to the landscape. The crop is grown in plenty of water, which reflects the sky and palms. The rice is harvested in late September.

This photograph of Anjuna Beach (below) *reflects its spirit—it is a beach for the adventurous and reckless, rather than for those who want to lie back in the sun. It is extremely popular with artists, defiant dropouts from the rat race and other 'alternative' people! There are several good seafood restaurants close by, catering to the many visitors to this spectacularly beautiful beach. Baga Beach* (right) *is a far more peaceful place, used by most as a kind of retreat, it can become crowded but is never chaotic.* (Bottom right) *seagulls at Calangute Beach. Calangute is a 7 km (4.3 miles) long beach which has been called, variously, 'the Queen of Goan beaches', 'paradise' and a 'den of iniquity'; it used to be a favourite hippy hang-out, but is now more a tourist haven. It is possible to shop here for trinkets and mementoes.*

Above
Another of Goa's famous white churches. This beautiful little building is a chapel near Aldona, which can be reached by launch from Panaji once a day.

Left
A Goan family makes an offering at a Cross outside the Church of the Immaculate Conception.

Above
The Manguesh Temple is 7.5 km (4.6 miles) away from Ponda; Sri Manguesha is, according to legend, a manifestation of the Lord Siva which was presented to his consort, Parvati, in response to her penance. The shrine dates back to 1565 but has been redone with huge chandeliers, probably a result of the Portuguese influence. The lamp tower is a feature unique to Goan temples.

Right
In contrast to the opulently carved temples, this small shrine in Old Goa possesses a simplicity of structure and design that is aesthetically most pleasing.

Following pages
Aguada beach resort is frequented by the richer tourists, and is known to be the jetsetters' favourite haunt. Named after Goa's most well-known fort, this five star resort is fully equipped with numerous fancy bars and restaurants. Despite all of this, it remains an extremely attractive beach.

Page 80
A Goan sunset is an experience not to be missed.

An A to Z of Facts and Figures

A

Airport Bombay's domestic airport, Santa Cruz, is about 26 km (16 miles) from the main city, while its international counterpart, Sahar airport lies 5 km (3 miles) beyond. The two airports are connected by frequently plying buses. Most of the airline offices are at Churchgate and Nariman Point. Indian Airlines and Air India booking offices are in the same building at Nariman Point.

Aquarium Near Chowpatty Beach, on Marine Drive, there are tanks of fresh water and salt water fish, as well as a section on the growth of a fish. The aquarium is well worth a visit, despite being uncomfortably crowded on holidays.

B

BEST The Bombay Electric Supply & Transport Undertaking runs Bombay's bus service. Though Bombayites complain, they are very proud of this service and are aware that it is the best city transport system in the country. It is cheap, efficient and manned by an army of extremely affable conductors.

Bhelpuri An inimitable Bombay mixture of *kurmura* (puffed rice), *sev* (made of chick-pea flour), *puris* (flat, crisp wafers made of wheat flour), onion, potato, chutneys and raw mango (if in season). Available almost anywhere in Bombay. *Sevpuri* is an equally delicious variant. (See also *panipuri*.)

Bombay Central If you come to Bombay by the Western Railway your train terminates at this railway station. It is extremely busy at all times since Bombay is the headquarters of the Western Railways.

Books Good English bookshops are not easy to find in Bombay. On Churchgate Street (Veer Nariman Road) and in parts of the Fort area, new and old books are sold on the pavement, often remainders at throwaway prices. Strand Book Stall on Pherozeshah Mehta Road and the new Bookpoint on Kamani Marg (Ballard Estate) are two fairly well-stocked bookshops. At Kalbadevi is the New and Secondhand Bookstore which is a treat for any book lover.

C

Chor Bazaar Literally 'Thieves Market', this is located at Mutton Street. Curios and quaint little collector's items make it worth exploring. Friday is the best day to visit as it is possible for the discerning visitor to pick up a genuine antique.

Chowpatty Beach This famous beach is typically Indian, rather dirty but also full of eccentricities. The beach is also the venue for the Ganesh Chaturthi festival.

Colaba Causeway Renamed Shahid Bhagat Singh Road, the Colaba Causeway extends to the southern end of Bombay island. Most of the cheaper hotels and restaurants are located here.

Crawford Market (Mahatma Phule Market) This is yet another of Bombay's seemingly inexhaustible bazaars. Fruit, vegetables, groceries, furniture, travel kits, hardware, crockery and pets can all be found here! There's even a smugglers' bazaar to satisfy the Bombayite's crave for 'phoren' goods.

Cricket Apart from the maidans, Bombay has two cricket stadiums which often host test matches. The Bombayite is a great lover of cricket and the game is played on every sidestreet of the city, often with a wooden plank used as the bat, an old tennis ball, and wickets drawn on a wall.

D

Dhobi Talao For sports enthusiasts, Dhobi Talao is a good place to shop since most of Bombay's main sports shops are found in this area. A large population of Goans have settled here.

E

Elephanta Caves About 10 km (6 miles) north-east from Apollo Bunder, Bombay's most famous tourist stop is the island of Elephanta. The rock-cut temples on the island are thought to date back to between AD 450 and 700. It is easy to reach but very crowded on weekends.

F

Flora Fountain Apart from being a beautiful structure, this fountain lends its name to the commercial heart of Bombay. It is where the most important banks and business offices are located. The Cathedral of St Thomas close by is worth a visit.

G

Ganesh Chaturthi This important Hindu festival is celebrated around August-September in Bombay. Ganesh (the elephant-headed god) is extremely popular in Maharashtra and the Siddhivinayaka temple dedicated to him at Prabhadevi draws huge crowds every Tuesday.

Gateway of India Bombay's very own Arc de Triumphe stands as a reminder of the European conquests of India. Officially opened in 1924, the Gateway—on Apollo Bunder Road—is Bombay's main landmark.

Goan food Traditional Konkanan ingredients of coconut milk, cashews, chilli and even mangoes are used with shrimps, fish, lobster and pork to make an exciting range of distinctly Goan dishes. Dishes such as *sorpotel*, a stew of pig's liver and pork marinated in vinegar; *vindaloo*, a hot pork curry; and the local sausage, *chorizo*, are all traditional favourites.

H

Hanging Gardens The Pherozeshah Mehta Gardens on top of Malabar Hill provide one of Bombay's few open spaces. Their more popular name is derived from the fact that they are built atop and trail over a large water supply tank.

I

Inquisition In Goa, the Inquisition tried over sixteen thousand people between 1561 and its dissolution in 1774. Agents of the Holy Office in other Portugese areas sent suspected heretics to Goa for trial. The heresies included any actions that continued to show signs of Hindu or Muslim influence, such as wearing a dhoti or refusing to eat pork.

J

Jehangir Art Gallery The best-known in Bombay, this gallery stands on the main museum complex and usually exhibits modern Indian art. Equipped with good facilities, the gallery houses the tiny but popular restaurant 'Samovar' which opens at 10.30 am.

Juhu Beach Situated 18 km (11 miles) away from the city centre, Juhu is close to the airport. It is far too polluted for a swim, but has the usual Bombay beach attractions which make for a rather carnival atmosphere.

K

Kalbadevi One of the busiest and most thickly populated commercial areas in the country, Kalbadevi is a must for any shopper. The goods offered range from cotton textiles to diamonds. It also has a number of cinema halls and video parlours.

Kamala Nehru Park Laid out in 1952, this park has beautiful views of the city. Children love its invitation to explore, especially in the 'Old Woman's Shoe' which is located here.

L

Libraries The grand old Asiatic Library, almost 200 years old, is housed in the Town Hall building. The British Council Library at Nariman Point attracts many of the younger Bombayites. The Bombay University Library and Petit Library are also popular.

M

Mahalaxmi Temple The oldest temple in Bombay, Mahalaxmi contains images of Laxmi, the goddess of wealth, which are supposed to have been discovered in the sea.

Maidans Large, open recreation grounds. There are three big maidans in South Bombay—the Oval Maidan, Cross Maidan and Azad Maidan. There are several others in central and north Bombay (see Shivaji Park). These green areas are much in demand, especially in the evenings and on holidays.

Marine Drive This road starts at Nariman Point and winds up on Malabar Hill. Many residential highrises are located on this famous promenade.

Mount Mary's Feast Celebrated on the 8th September every year at Mount Mary's Church in Bandra. The week-long Bandra Fair starts on the first Sunday of the Feast. People of all faiths flock to the church to seek favours through Mother Mary.

N

Nariman Point This is the part of Bombay which most often inspires comparisons with Manhattan. The cluster of skyscrapers houses some of the most important business offices in the city along with plush flats, and expensive restaurants.

NCPA The National Centre for the Performing Arts at Nariman Point. This complex includes the impressive Tata Theatre.

Nehru Centre Located on Lala Lajpat Rai Marg, the centre consists of the Nehru Science Museum with its superlative children's section and sound and light show. The Nehru Planetarium is also one of the best in the country and a big crowd-puller.

P

Panipuri Unlike Bhelpuris, these snacks are puffed up and hollow. A hole is made in one side and the puri is filled up with tangy *pani* (which contains plenty of spices and tamarind) and sprouted gram. Handed out one at a time, these puris are tasty morsels which leave you refreshed and tingling.

Pau-bhaji If you're really hungry try this spicy mixture of vegetables cooked in butter, eaten with *pau* (bread) also lightly fried in butter. It is a traditional Gujerati dish which has become a favourite snack in Bombay.

Prince of Wales Museum Built for King George V's first visit to India as the Prince of Wales, the museum is located beside the Wellington Circle. Sections on art, archaeology and natural history have abundant displays which help make it an extremely informative museum.

Q

Queen's Necklace Marine Drive sweeps around Chowpatty Beach in a lovely curve. At night, when seen from Malabar Hill, the curve of street lights resembles a glowing pearl string—the 'Queen's Necklace'.

R

Raj Bhavan One of the few really old buildings left in Bombay, the Governor's house has a beautiful view from the promontory where it is located. It has a private beach at the foot of Malabar Hill.

Rabindra Natya Mandir Like the Prithvi Theatre and Shivaji Mandir, this is the venue for much of Bombay's local vernacular theatre.

Rang Bhavan In the Dhobi Talao area, this theatre is the venue for most large concerts of Indian and popular Western music in Bombay. It also stages Marathi plays, and the traditional folk *tamasha* shows

S

Sahitya Sangh This new cinema house was recently set up to promote high quality films, from India and other countries.

Shivaji Park A major *maidan* with about half a dozen cricket pitches where many of India's test cricketers have honed their skills. It is also used to hold political rallies, which are noisy, ill-managed and often get out of control.

Stock Exchange The skyscraper which houses India's stock exchange stands on Dalal (Brokers') Street. It is the scene of noisy trade both inside and on the pavements outside. Architecturally quite remarkable, it affords a marvellous view of Bombay's business district and the port from the top of the building.

T

Tatas An important Parsi industrialist family, the Tatas hail from Bombay. The city has benefited greatly from the philanthropy of this family; examples include the Tata Institute of Fundamental Research, the Tata Memorial Hospital, the Tata Institute of Social Sciences and the Tata Theatre.

V

Victoria Terminus 'VT' is an enormous and elaborate Gothic building which is the terminus for the Central Railway trains. Today it seethes with activity since almost half a million commuters use it every day.

X

Xavier St Francis Xavier arrived in Goa in 1542 and worked for a year in a seminary before moving east to Malacca and Japan. After an unsuccessful attempt to establish a mission to China, he died off the Chinese coast in 1552. Two years later his body was returned to Goa. In 1636 it was placed in a locally made silver casket and kept in a side chapel off the Basilica of Bom Jesus.

Z

Zoo Along with the Victoria and Albert Museum, the zoo is set in what was originally called the Victoria Gardens, but is now known as the Veermata Jijabai Bhonsle Udyan. It is open from sunrise to sunset but has its limitations since the collection of animals is not very large.

INDEX

GS/12/01